Step by Step

Piano Course

by

Edna Mae Burnam

To my wonderful friends

ISBN 978-1-4234-3591-4

WILLIS MUSIC

EXCLUSIVELY DISTRIBUTED BY

7777 W. BLUEMOUND RD. P.O. BOX 13819 MILWAUKEE, WI 53213

Visit Hal Leonard Online at
www.halleonard.com

TO THE TEACHER

This is Book Six of Edna Mae Burnam's Piano Course—STEP BY STEP.

It is designed to follow her Book Five by showing new subjects in logical order, and one at a time.

Sufficient work is given on each step so that the student will thoroughly comprehend it before going on to the next step.

The meaning of all musical words and expression marks used in the book is given on pages 57 and 58.

When the student completes Book Six the following will have been learned:—

1. Key Signatures—

   a. How to read and play in the following **new** key signatures:

B major	D-flat major	A-flat major
F-sharp major	G-flat major	
C-sharp major	C-flat major	

   b. How to read and play more pieces in key signatures used in Books One, Two, Three, Four, and Five.

2. How to change fingers on repeated notes.

3. How to count and play dotted eighth notes.

4. How to read and play grace notes.

5. How to understand and recognize half steps.

6. How to analyze, finger correctly, and play chromatic passages and chromatic scales.

7. How to understand, read, and play a white key used as a sharp and a white key used as a flat.

8. How to read and play rolled chords.

9. How to read and play music written on three staves.

10. How to recognize the sign ₵ and to count and play *alla breve*.

11. How to play six-eight meter twice as fast and count it two counts to each measure.

12. How to play a piece with right hand having melody in middle and left hand crossing back and forth over right for accompaniment.

13. How to recognize the sign *tr*〜〜〜 and to play a trill.

14. How to recognize the sign ∾ and to play a turn.

15. To know the correct pronunciation and meaning of the following musical words and signs:

WORDS	SIGNS
accel.	$>$
andante	$<$
andantino	$>$
animato	f
alla breve	mf
allegretto	ff
allegro	p
cresc.	mp
dim.	pp
dolce	$\frown$
fine	‿
gai	.
giocoso	$\overset{\frown}{3}$
legato	**C**
lésto	**¢**
marcato	*R. H.*
moderato	*L. H.*
pedal simile	*D. C. al fine*
poco	:‖
poco a poco cresc.	8-------
simile	⌊_____⌋
staccato	
staccato simile	
tempo	
tempo di marcia	
ritard.	

CHANGING FINGERS ON REPEATED NOTES

Notice the finger markings on the repeated notes.

Use a quick finger staccato.

Pluck the notes as you would pluck a banjo string.

Use the correct fingering.

Giocoso means "merrily".

POLKA DOTS

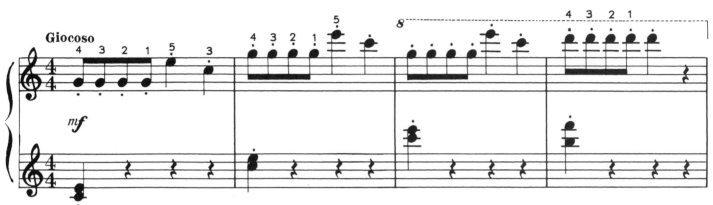

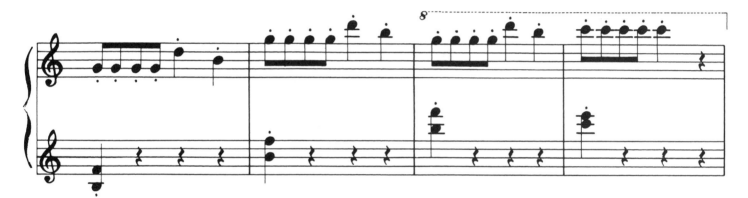

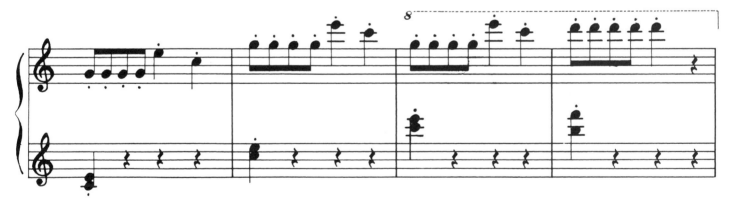

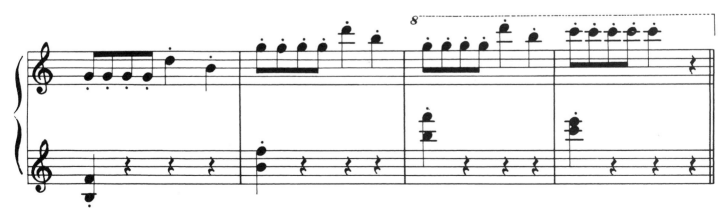

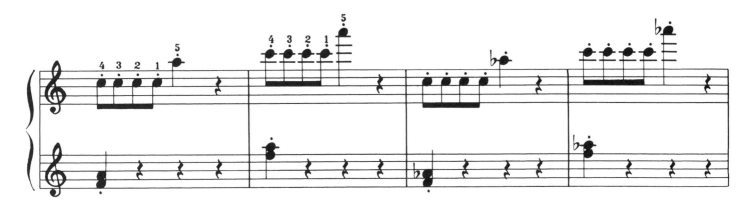

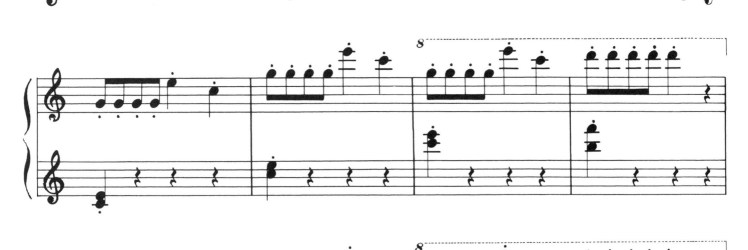

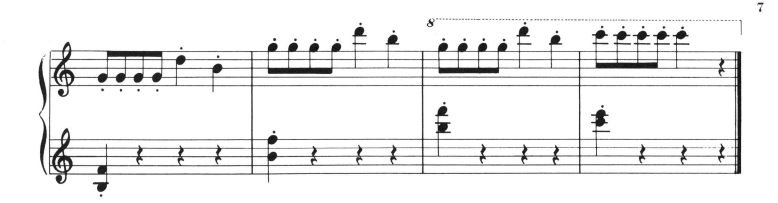

DOTTED EIGHTH NOTE

A dot placed after a note adds to that note one half of its value.

You have learned this with a quarter note.

The same is true of an eighth note.

A dotted eighth note is usually followed by a sixteenth note to complete the unfinished part of the count.

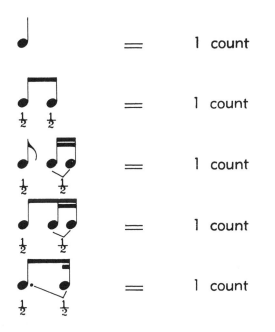

When an eighth note is dotted, the sixteenth note that follows skips quickly to the next count.

It really sounds like music for skipping! Stand up and try skipping around the room a few steps to get the "feel" of the time. Now play and count this exercise.

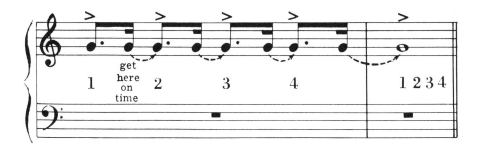

BATTLE HYMN OF THE REPUBLIC

Julia Ward Howe

William Steffe
Arr. by E. M. Burnam

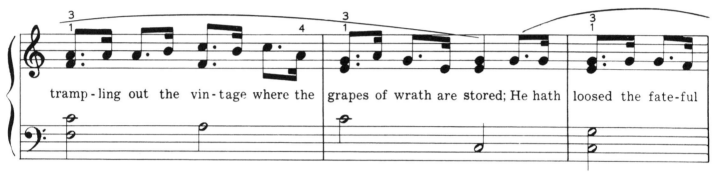

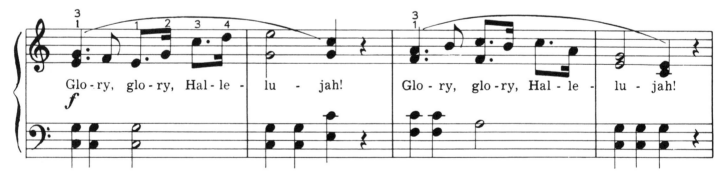

JOGGIN' ALONG IN AN OLD STAGECOACH

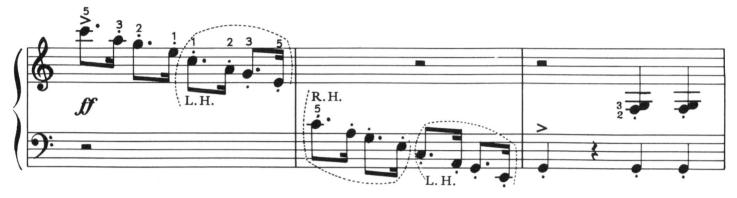

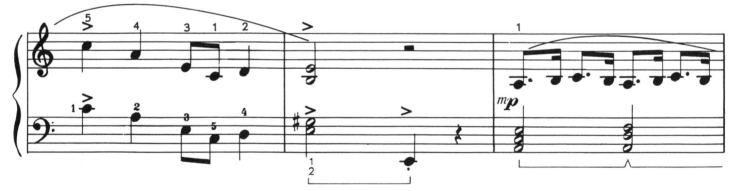

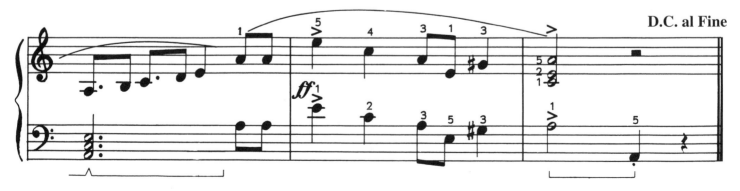

KEY OF B MAJOR

Notice the key signature of this piece. This is the key of B major.

There are five sharps.

Remember to sharp every F, C, G, D, and A as you play this piece.

A PRISM LANTERN IN THE SUN

GRACE NOTES

There are several kinds of grace notes.

The one used most often is the short grace note, and it looks like this

This kind of grace note has no time value, so it is not part of the count.

The note which **follows** the grace note receives the count.

The grace note "snips" quickly to the note that receives the count.

The principal note may be higher than
the grace note like this:

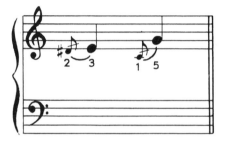

or

lower than the grace note like this:

In the following piece the second finger is used on every grace note—and every grace note is a black key.

In the last line of the piece, every black key is used as you move down the keyboard!

SANDPIPER ON THE BEACH

Lésto means—lively, quick, nimble.

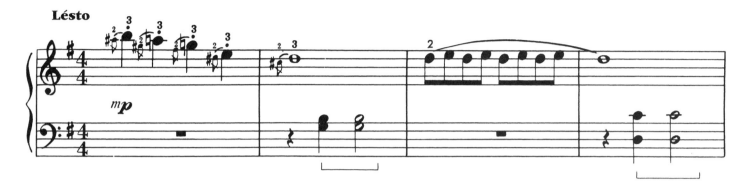

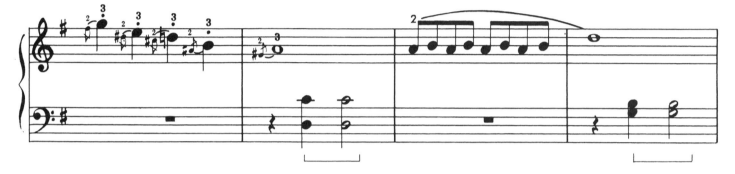

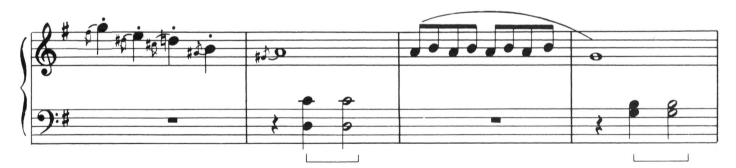

SPRING IS IN THE AIR

Gai means "gay" or "happy".

Pedal simile—keep pedaling in the same manner.

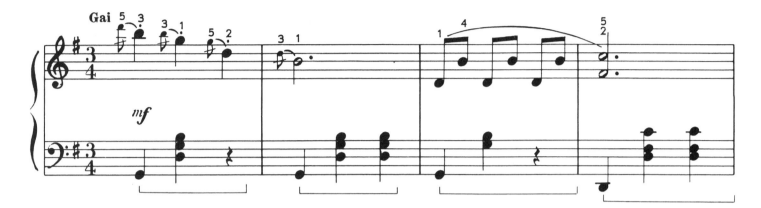

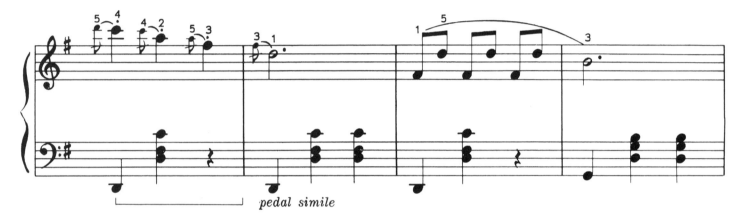

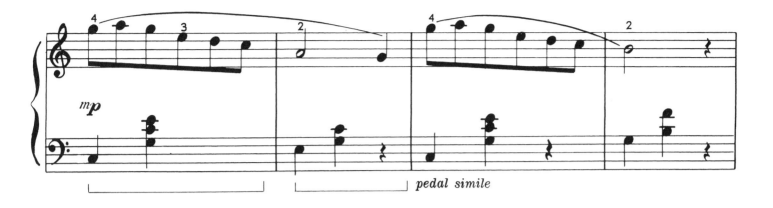

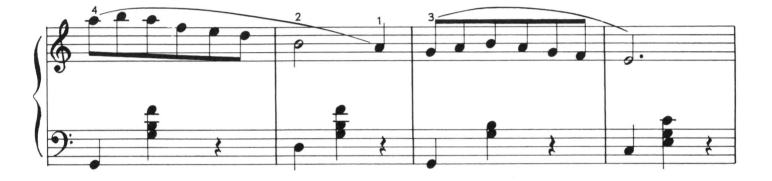

Sometimes several grace notes are used to "roll" into a note that receives the count. Think of a drum roll as you play the grace notes in the next piece.

Notice the fourth count of the fourth measure. These are **not** grace notes. It is a triplet — and should be counted as a triplet (four-trip-let.)

AMERICAN PATROL
March

F. W. Meacham
Arr. by E. M. Burnam

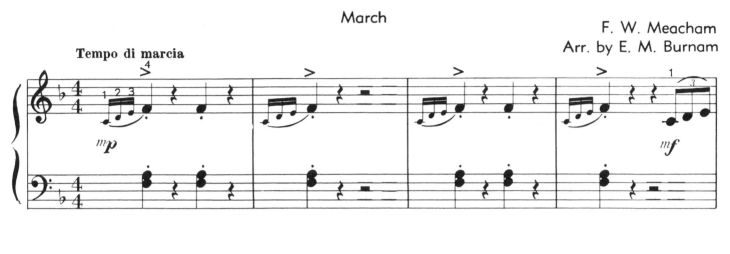

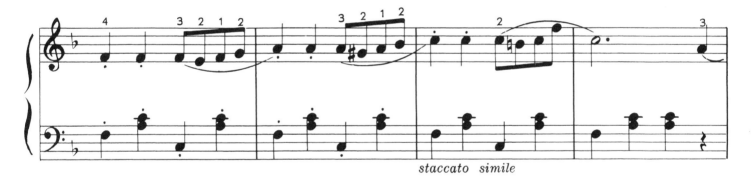

staccato simile

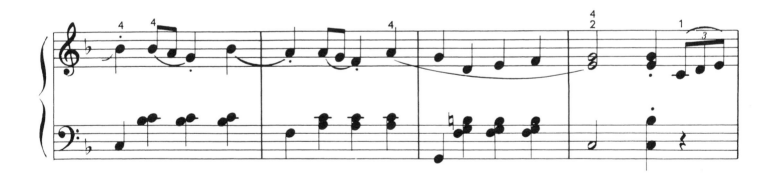

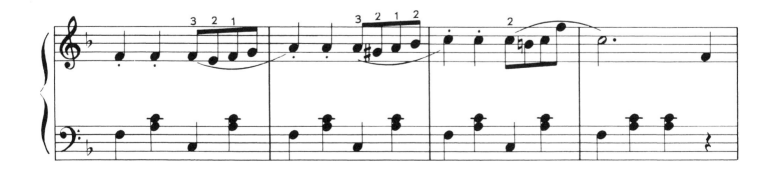

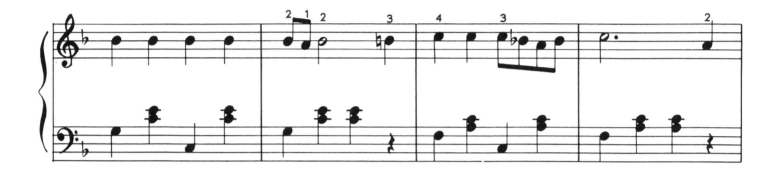

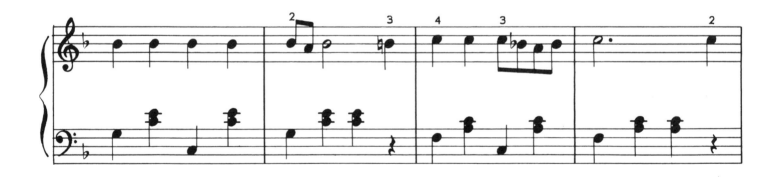

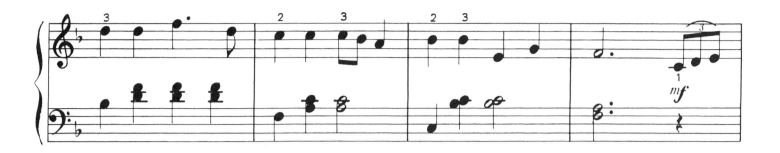

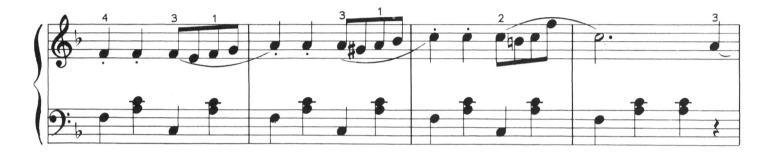

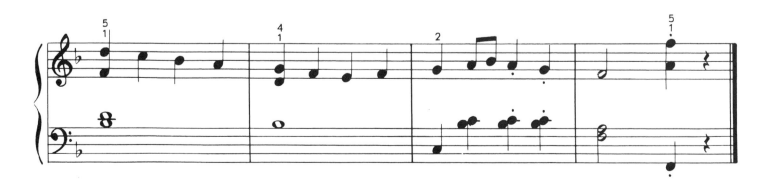

HALF STEPS

The distance between any key and the next nearest key up, or down, is a half step.

A half step is the **shortest** distance we can move up or down on the piano keyboard.

Here is a half step up.

Here is a half step down.

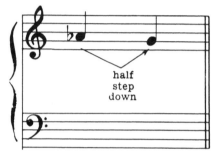

Usually a half step is from a white key to a black key or a black key to a white key, but there are two places in the musical alphabet where a half step is from a white key to another white key. These are between E and F and between B and C.

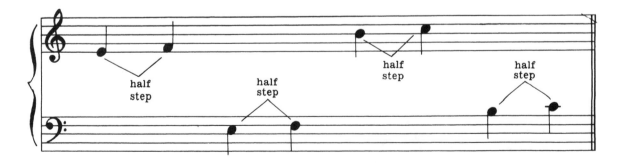

CHROMATIC PASSAGES

A series of consecutive half steps moving up or down is a chromatic passage.

In a chromatic passage the third finger should be used on every black key — and only fingers 1, 2, and 3 are used.

Play the following chromatic passages—using the fingering indicated.

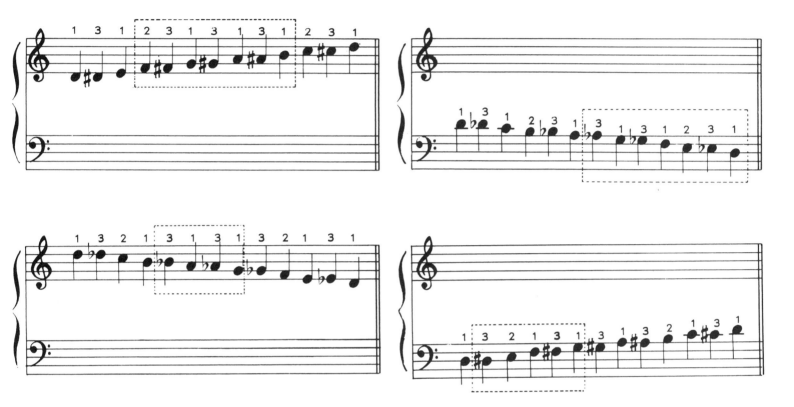

Wherever you begin, use the **same** fingering.

Now just play the notes in the **little boxes** in the above examples.

This will show you how you may always use the same fingering no matter where you begin.

THE CHROMATIC SCALE

The chromatic scale is composed of twelve consecutive half steps — moving up or down. (This is one octave). You may begin a chromatic scale on any note. **Wherever** you begin, use the same fingering. Using your right hand, play a chromatic scale from F-sharp up to F-sharp. Using your left hand, play a chromatic scale from A down to A.

Using your right hand, play a chromatic scale beginning on middle C — going up to the highest C on the keyboard—then back to middle C.

Using your left hand, play a chromatic scale beginning on middle C — going down to the lowest C on the keyboard—then back to middle C.

The following piece has some chromatic passages.

A SOFT WIND

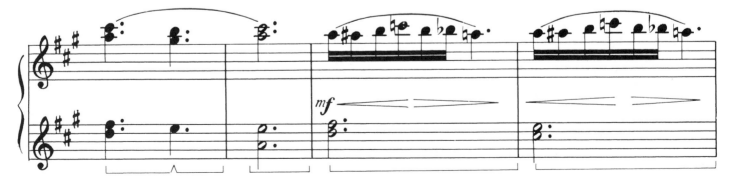

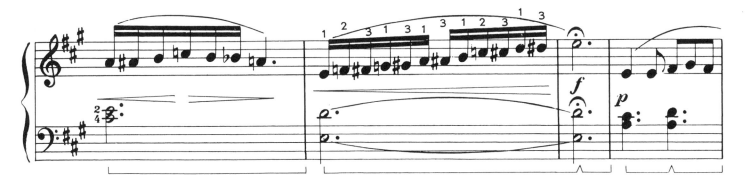

KEY OF B-FLAT MAJOR

There are two flats in the key signature of B-Flat Major.

The flats to remember are B and E.

HOPPITY

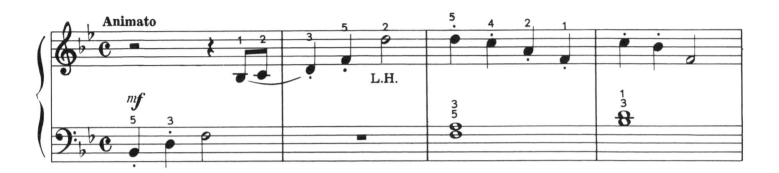

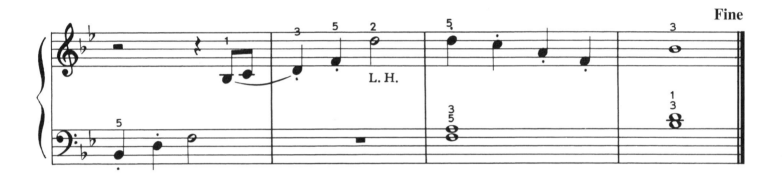

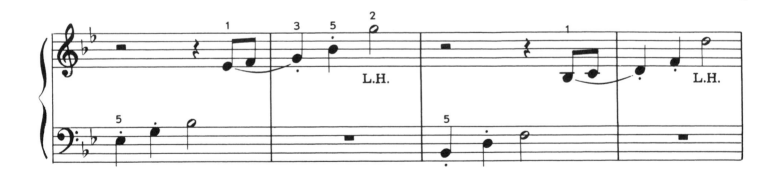

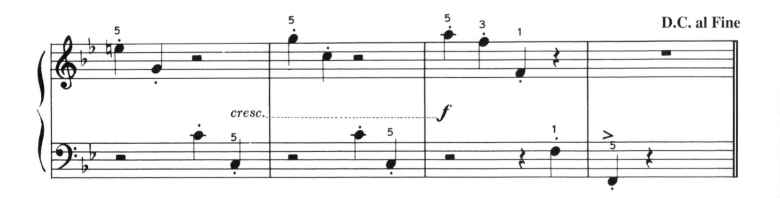

TELL ME WHY

American College Song

Arranged by E. M. Burnam

A WHITE KEY CAN BE A SHARP
A WHITE KEY CAN BE A FLAT

When we sharp or flat a note we usually move up or down a half step to a black key. But where the two white keys come together as a half step, there is no black key to move to—so the sharp must be a white key.

Play F

Play F-sharp

Play F again

Play F-flat (a white key)

Play E

Play E-flat

Play E again

Play E-sharp (a white key)

Play C

Play C-sharp

Play C again

Play C-flat (a white key)

Play B

Play B-flat

Play B again

Play B-sharp (a white key)

The next piece uses a white key as a sharp several times.

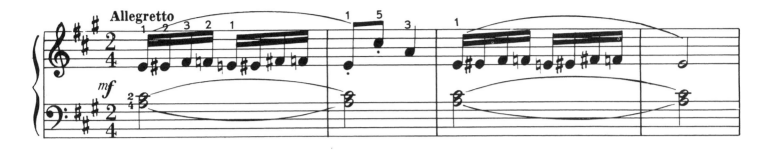

SONG OF THE BEE

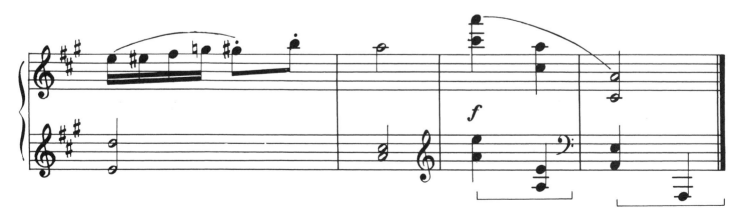

KEY OF F-SHARP MAJOR

Notice the key signature of this piece.

This is the key of F-sharp major.

There are six sharps.

The sharps are F, C, G, D, A, E.

MOONLIGHT MUSIC

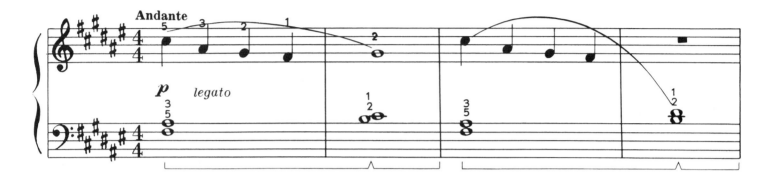

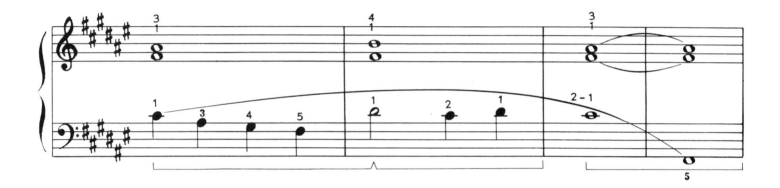

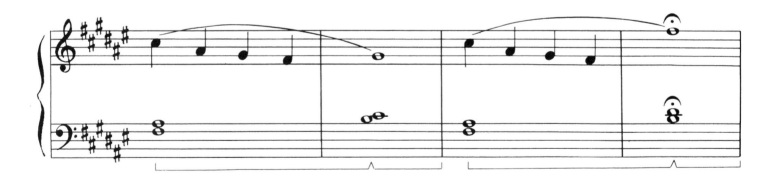

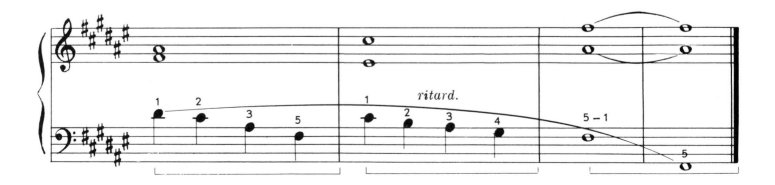

ROLLED CHORDS

When a chord has a curved line like this ![chord symbol] just before it, the chord should be rolled. This means the notes should be played quickly—one at a time from the bottom note to the top note—and each note is held down as it is played.

When there is a rolled line for the chord in each hand, they should be played at the same time.

play like this

When there is a long unbroken roll line for both hands, the chords should be played this way:

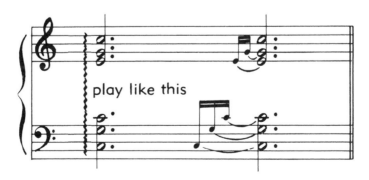

play like this

NIGHT SONG

(Nocturne)

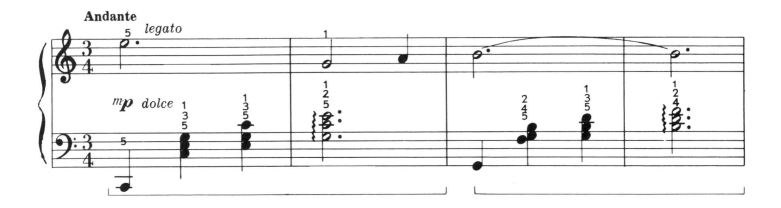

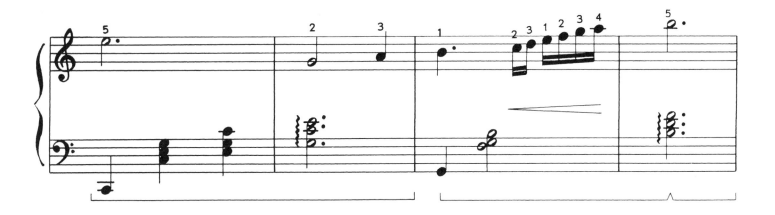

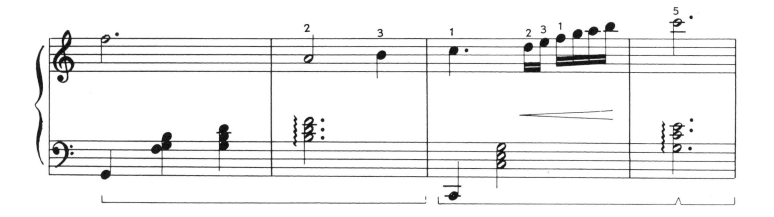

READING ON THREE STAVES

Sometimes, for convenience in reading, music is written on three staves.

In the following piece the rolled chord is held by the pedal, as the right hand plays the music on the staff above.

DAY DREAMING

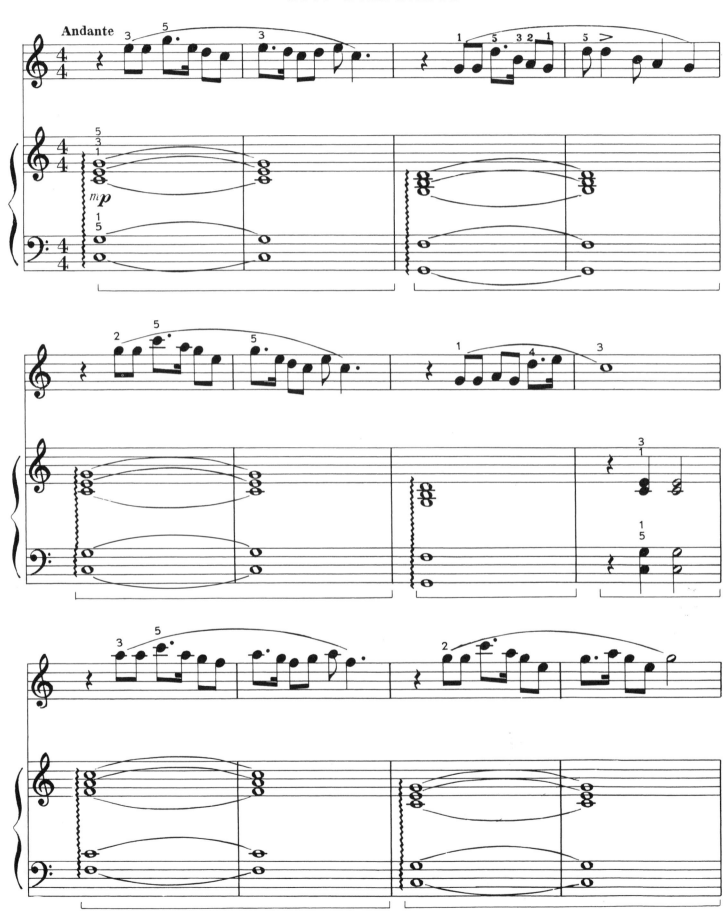

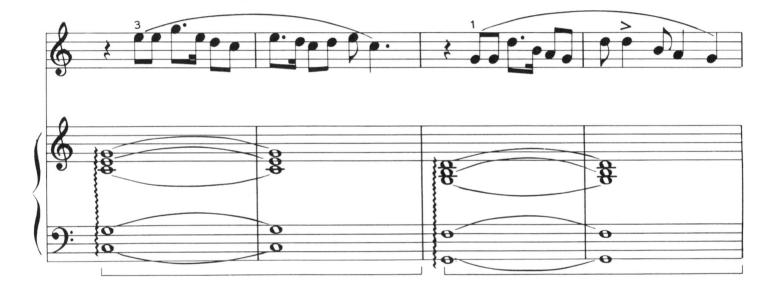

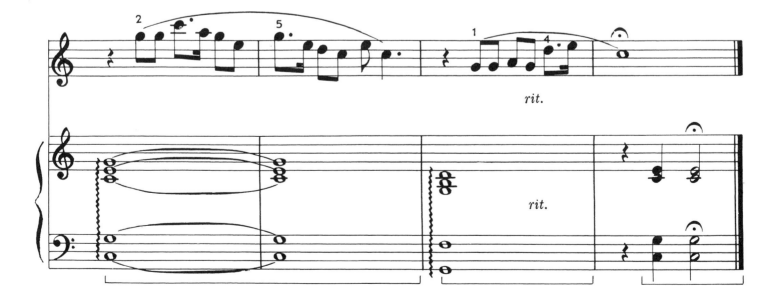

ALLA BREVE

You have learned that a sign like this **C** means four-four meter. When you see this sign with a line through it—like this **¢** it is called alla breve.

The alla breve sign does not change the rhythm of the piece. It means the piece should be played **twice as fast.** Instead of counting four counts to a measure (which would be hard to do at this speed) it should be counted two counts to a measure.

First learn the piece in four-
four meter and count and play
this way:

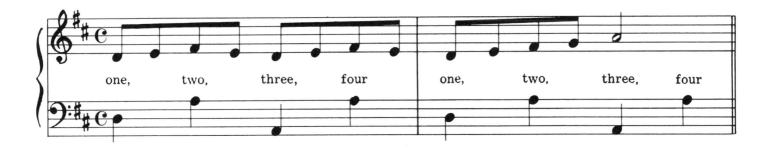

Then, as speed develops,
change to alla breve, and play
and count it this way:

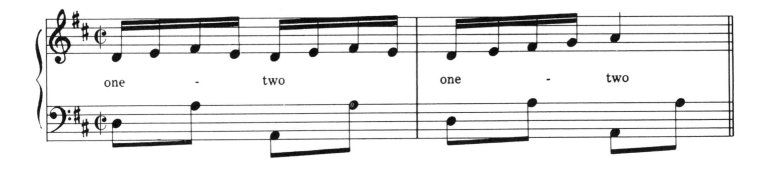

RINGS AND CIRCLES

KEY OF C-SHARP MAJOR

Notice the key signature of this piece.
This is the key of C-sharp major.
There are seven sharps.
The sharps are F, C, G, D, A, E, B.

ROSES BY MY WINDOW

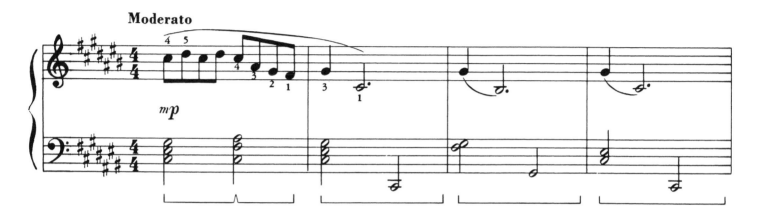

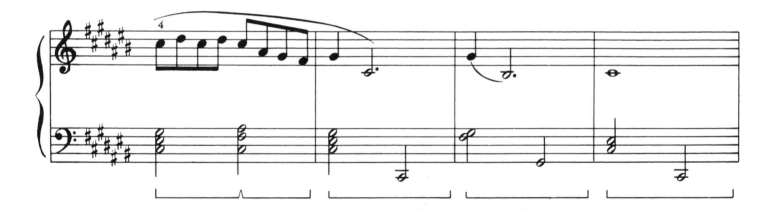

KEY OF A-FLAT MAJOR

Notice the key signature of this piece.

This is the key of A-flat major.

There are four flats.

The flats are B, E, A, D.

A MORNING IN THE HILLS

KEY OF D-FLAT MAJOR

Notice the key signature of this piece.

This is the key of D-flat major.

There are five flats.

The flats to remember are B, E, A, D, G.

A LULLABY

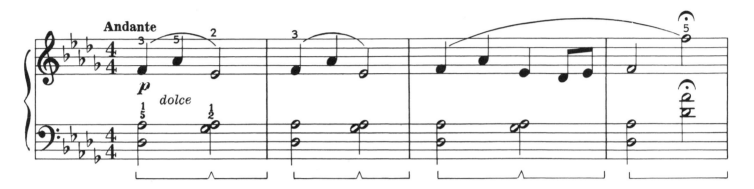

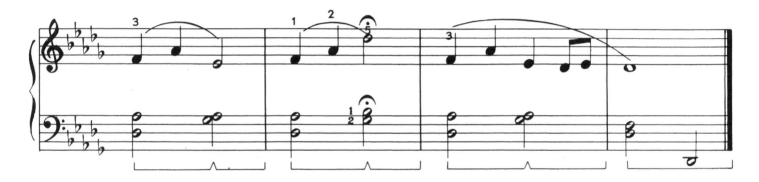

KEY OF G-FLAT MAJOR

Notice the key signature of this piece.

This is the key of G-flat major.

There are six flats.

The flats to remember are B, E, A, D, G, C.

A LOVELY CHINESE MAIDEN

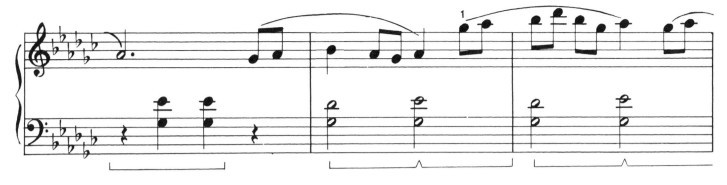

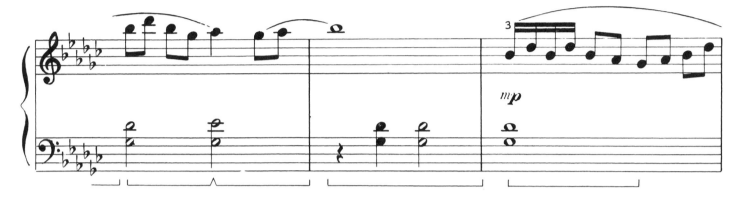

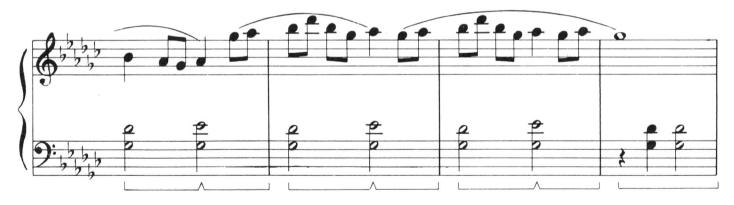

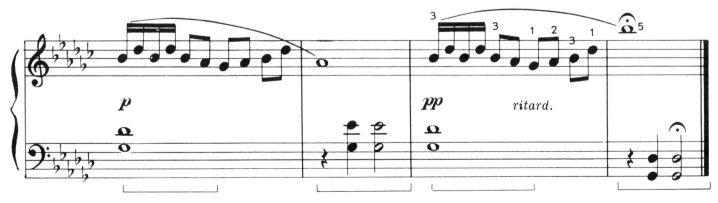

KEY OF C-FLAT MAJOR

There are seven flats in the key of C-Flat Major.

The flats to remember are B, E, A, D, G, C, F.

C-flat is a **white key**—and F-flat is a **white key.**

Play C-flat and F-flat before you begin.

QUIET THOUGHTS

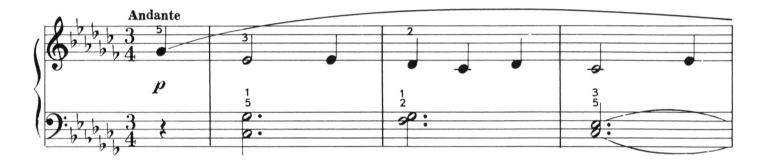

COUNT SIX-EIGHT METER IN TWO COUNTS FOR SPEED

You have learned that you may play four-four meter twice as fast and count two to a measure.

It is also easy to change the counting in six-eight meter.

When a piece in six-eight meter is to be played at a fast tempo, it is easier to count it two counts to a measure (Think of it as two triplets to each measure).

First learn the piece counting six
to each measure like this:

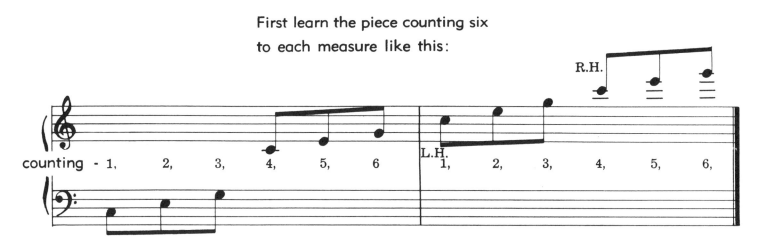

Then, as speed develops, change
and count this way:

The next piece in six-eight meter should be played at a lively tempo, so when the notes are learned—and as speed develops—change and count two to each measure.

SERPENTINE AND CONFETTI

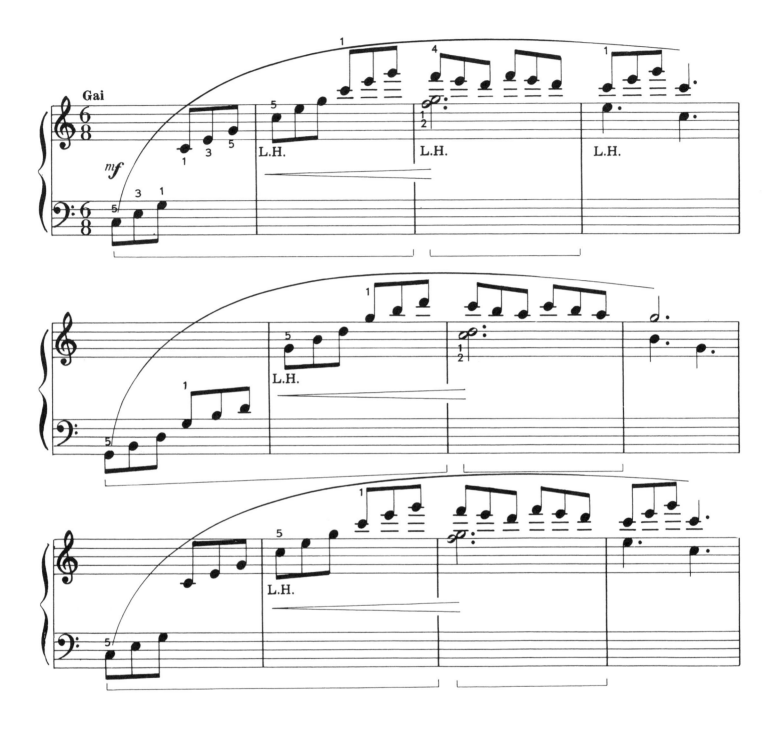

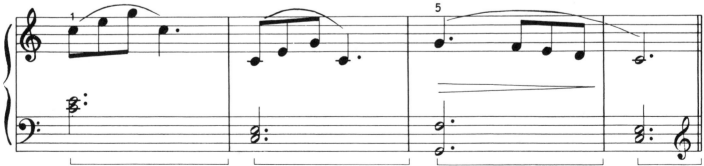

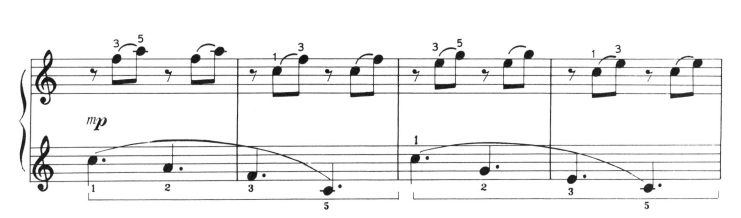

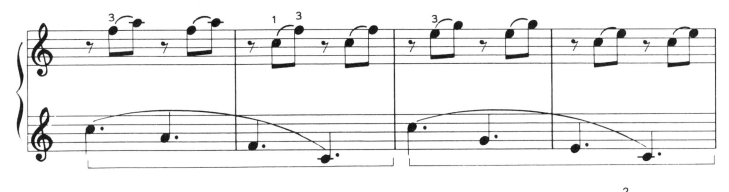

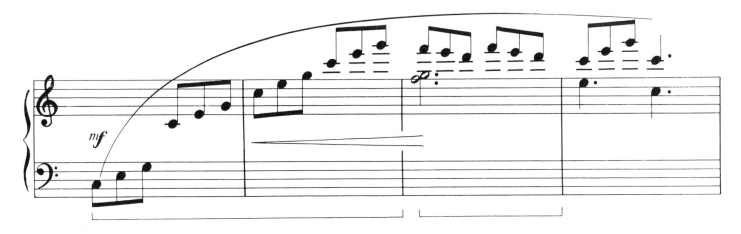

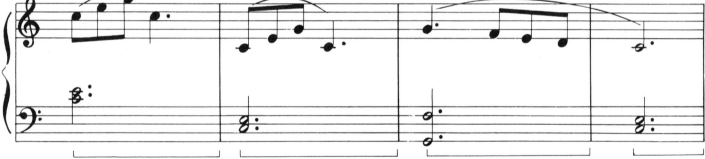

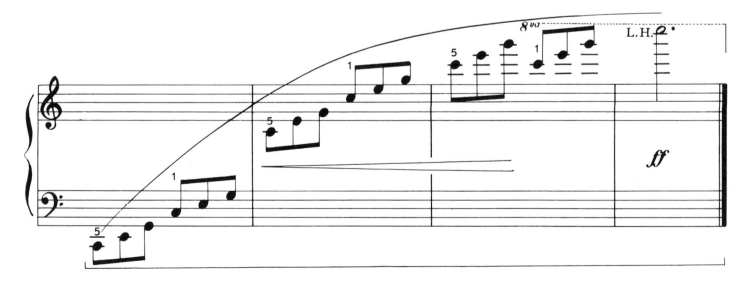

LEFT HAND CROSSES BACK AND FORTH
RIGHT HAND PLAYS MELODY

The melody (or song part) of this piece is played by the right hand.

Practice the melody part first—like this:

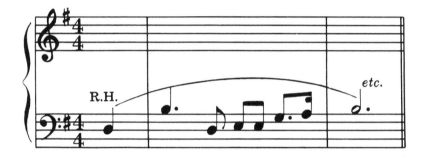

The left hand plays the low notes and all of the chords.

Practice the left-hand part like this:

(Left hand plays all of this.)

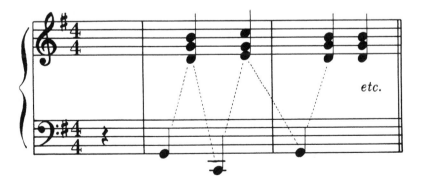

GRANDMOTHER'S MEMORIES

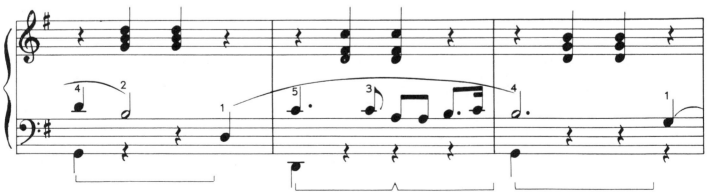

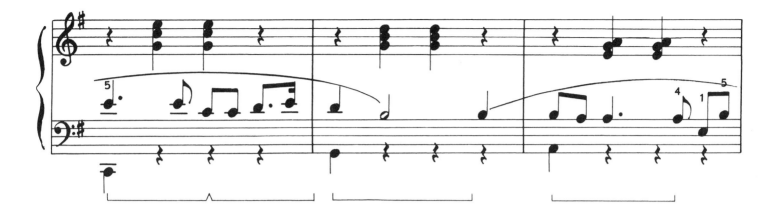

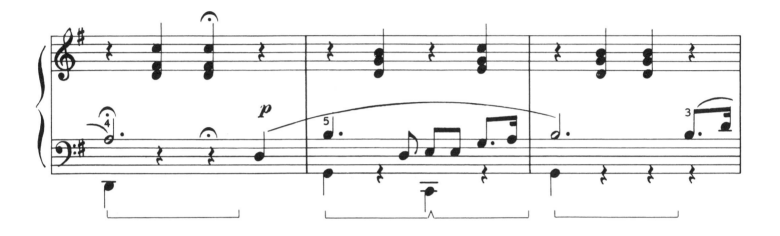

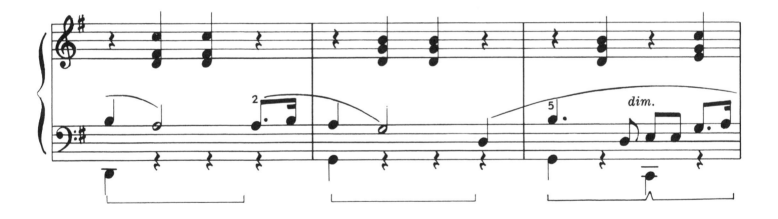

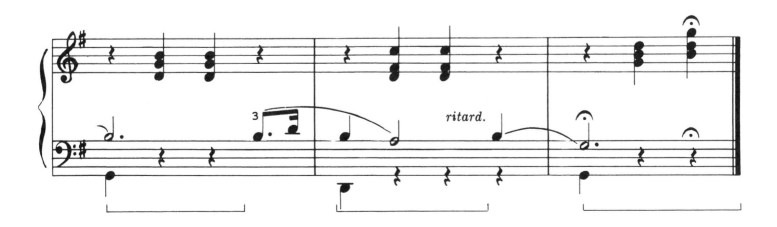

THE TRILL

A trill is two adjacent notes alternating in rapid succession like this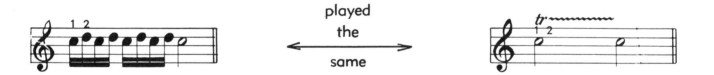

The sign of the trill is

When a trill sign is placed over a note, it means this note and the note above are to be alternated for the time value of the note.

The two following examples are played exactly the same:

played
the
same

In the next piece **some** of the trill figures have the notes completely written out—but some of them have the trill sign.

TO A LITTLE BIRD

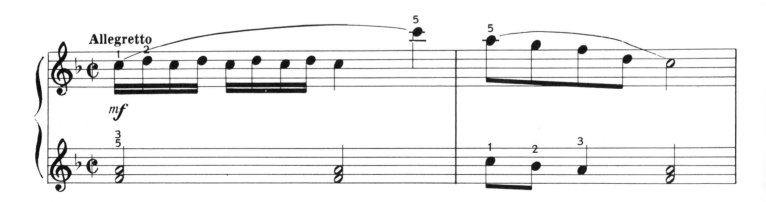

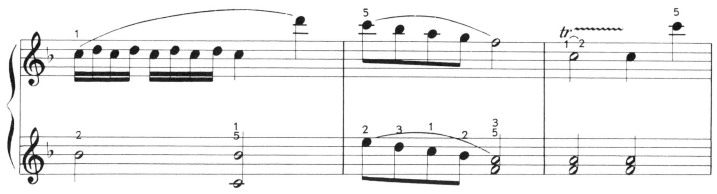

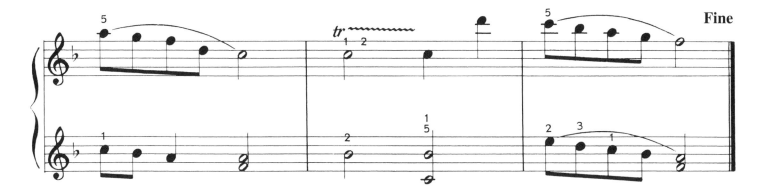

Fine

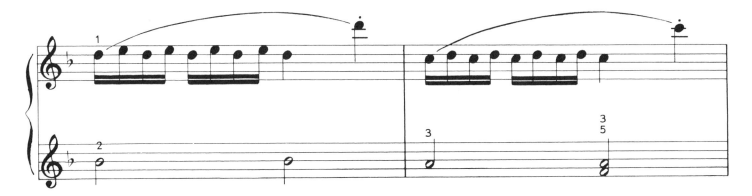

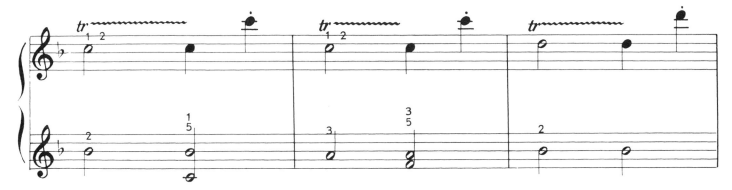

D.C. al Fine

REFLECTIONS

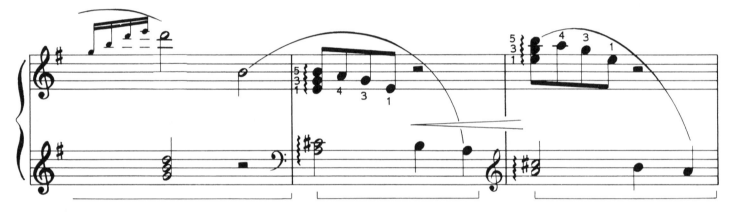

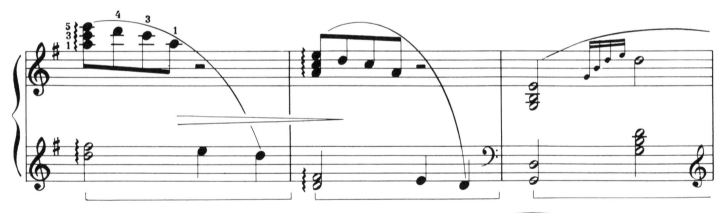

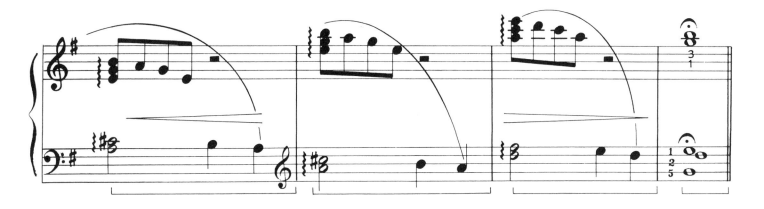

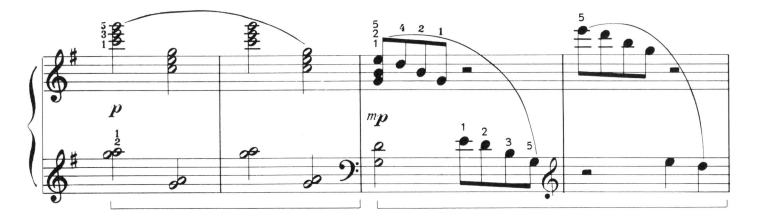

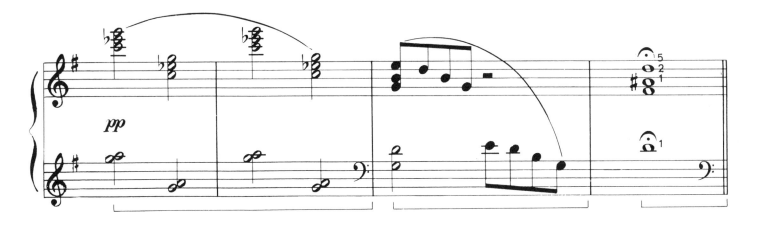

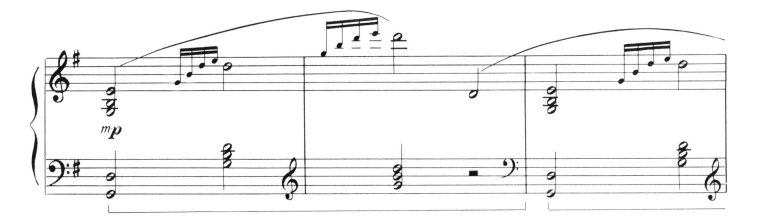

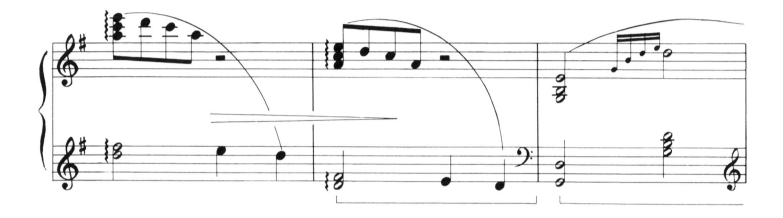

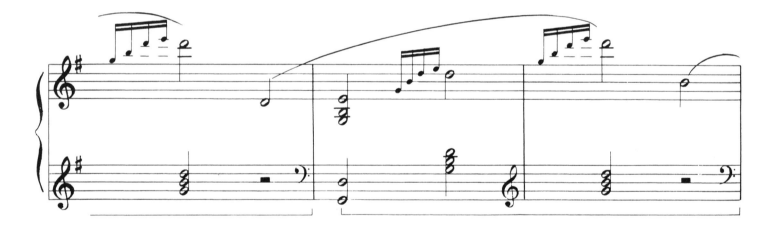

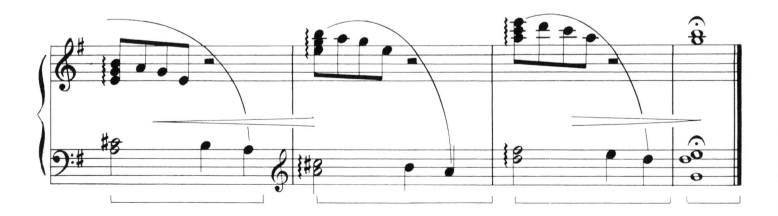

The turn is a group of rapid ornamental notes connecting one principal note to another like this:

The sign of the turn is placed over a note like this:

When the sign is present the turn should be filled in.

Very often the finger marks of the turn are printed—like this:

The following piece has some turns written out, and some are indicated by the sign of the turn.

RED RIBBON BOWS

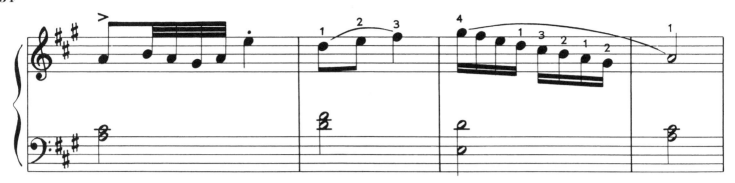
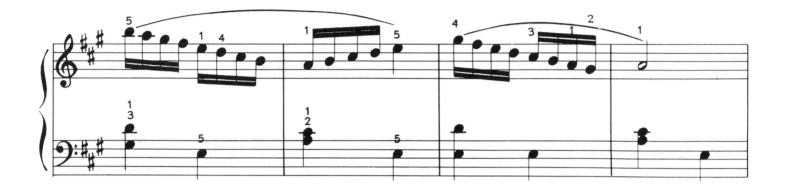

MARCH ALONG MARCH

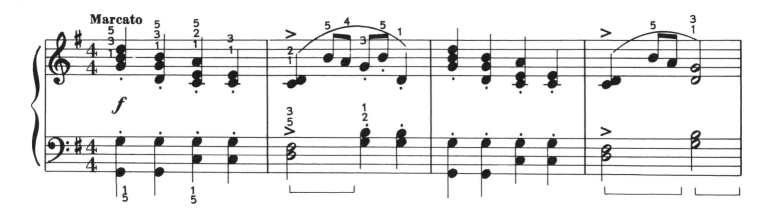

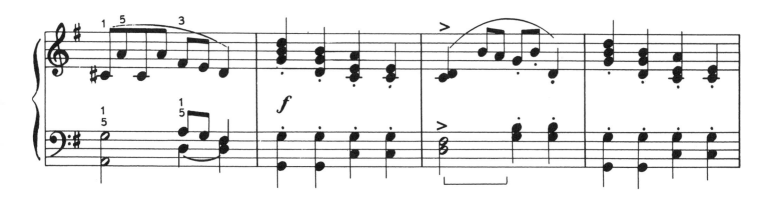

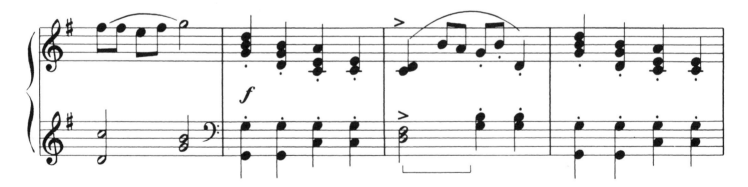

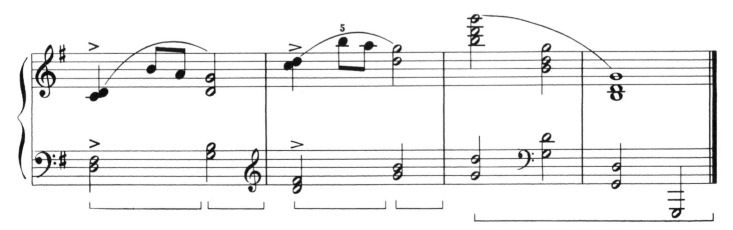

MUSICAL WORDS AND EXPRESSION MARKS
USED IN THIS BOOK

WORDS

accel. (accelerando)—gradually faster

andante—slow

andantino—a little slower than andante

animato—with life and spirit

alla breve—twice as fast   (see page 34, "Rings and Circles")

allegretto—light and lively, but not as quick as allegro

allegro—rapid, quick, lively

cresc. (crescendo)—gradually louder

dim. (diminuendo)—gradually softer

dolce—softly and sweetly

fine—the end

gai—gay

giocoso—merrily

legato—smooth and connected

lésto—lively, nimble, quick

marcato—march time

moderato—moderately fast

pedal simile—keep pedaling in the same manner

poco—little

poco a poco cresc.—little by little gradually louder

simile—in the same manner

staccato—short and detached

staccato simile—keep staccato in the same manner

tempo—time

tempo di marcia—time of a march

ritard.—gradually slower

SIGNS

>	— accent: emphasis on note or chord
⏷	— gradually louder
⏵	— gradually softer
f	— loud (forte)
mf	— moderately loud (mezzo forte)
ff	— very loud (fortissimo)
p	— soft (piano)
mp	— moderately soft (mezzo piano)
pp	— very soft (pianissimo)
⌢	— hold note longer
R. H.	— right hand
L. H.	— left hand
⌣	— slur: connected
·	— staccato: short, detached
3	— triplet: three notes get one count
C	— another sign for four-four meter
¢	— sign for alla breve (see page 34, "Rings and Circles")
D. C. al fine	— repeat from beginning and play to "fine"
:‖	— repeat
8------	— octave higher
⌊____⌋	— pedal

Certificate of Merit

This is to certify that

_____

has successfully completed

STEP BY STEP
BY
EDNA MAE BURNAM

_____Teacher

Date _____

Edna Mae Burnam was a pioneer in piano publishing. The creator of the iconic *A Dozen a Day* technique series and *Step by Step* method was born on September 15, 1907 in Sacramento, California. She began lessons with her mother, a piano teacher who drove a horse and buggy daily through the Sutter Buttes mountain range to reach her students. In college Burnam decided that she too enjoyed teaching young children, and majored in elementary education at California State University (then Chico State College) with a minor in music. She spent several years teaching kindergarten in public schools before starting her own piano studio and raising daughters Pat and Peggy. She delighted in composing for her students, and took theory and harmony lessons from her husband David (a music professor and conductor of the Sacramento Symphony in the 1940s).

Burnam began submitting original pieces to publishers in the mid-1930s, and was thrilled when one of them, "The Clock That Stopped," was accepted, even though her remuneration was a mere $20. Undaunted, the industrious composer sent in the first *A Dozen a Day* manuscript to her Willis editor in 1950, complete with stick-figure sketches for each exercise. Her editor loved the simple genius of the playful artwork resembling a musical technique, and so did students and teachers: the book rapidly blossomed into a series of seven and continues to sell millions of copies. In 1959, the first book in the *Step by Step* series was published, with hundreds of individual songs and pieces along the way, often identified by whimsical titles in Burnam's trademark style.

The immense popularity of her books solidified Edna Mae Burnam's place and reputation in music publishing history, yet throughout her lifetime she remained humble and effervescent. "I always left our conversations feeling upbeat and happy," says Kevin Cranley, Willis president. "She could charm the legs off a piano bench," Bob Sylva of the *Sacramento Bee* wrote, "make a melody out of a soap bubble, and a song out of a moon beam."

Burnam died in 2007, a few months shy of her 100th birthday. "Music enriches anybody's life, even if you don't turn out to be musical," she said once in an interview. "I can't imagine being in a house without a piano."

A DOZEN A DAY

by *Edna Mae Burnam*

The **A Dozen A Day** books are universally recognized as one of the most remarkable technique series on the market for all ages! Each book in this series contains short warm-up exercises to be played at the beginning of each practice session, providing excellent day-to-day training for the student. All book/audio versions include orchestrated accompaniments by Ric Ianonne.

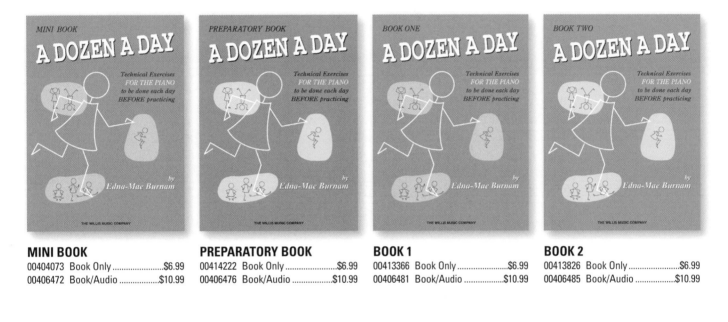

MINI BOOK
00404073 Book Only $6.99
00406472 Book/Audio $10.99

PREPARATORY BOOK
00414222 Book Only $6.99
00406476 Book/Audio $10.99

BOOK 1
00413366 Book Only $6.99
00406481 Book/Audio $10.99

BOOK 2
00413826 Book Only $6.99
00406485 Book/Audio $10.99

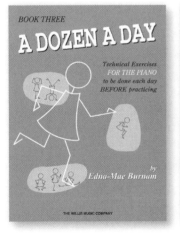
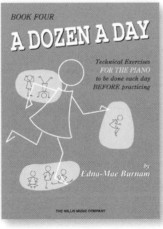
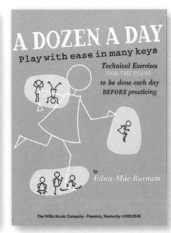
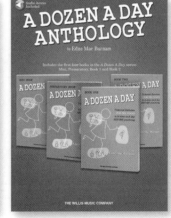

BOOK 3
00414136 Book Only $7.99
00416760 Book/Audio $10.99

BOOK 4
00415686 Book Only $7.99
00416761 Book/Audio $11.99

**PLAY WITH EASE
IN MANY KEYS**
00416395 Book Only $6.99

**A DOZEN A DAY
ANTHOLOGY**
00158307 Book/Audio $25.99

WILLIS MUSIC

EXCLUSIVELY DISTRIBUTED BY

HAL•LEONARD®

Prices, contents, and availability subject to change without notice. Prices listed in U.S. funds.